*Barrow Hills School
Senior Library*

Rainy Weather

Written by Jillian Powell

Wayland

The Weather

Rainy Weather
Snowy Weather
Sunny Weather
Windy Weather

First published in 1992 by
Wayland (Publishers) Ltd
61, Western Road, Hove
East Sussex BN3 1JD, England

© Copyright 1992 Wayland (Publishers) Ltd

Editor: Francesca Motisi
Designer: Joyce Chester

British Library Cataloguing in Publication Data
  Powell, Jillian
  Rainy Weather – (Weather Series)
  I. Title II. Series
  551.57

  ISBN 0-7502-0505-9

Typeset by Dorchester Typesetting Group Ltd.
Printed in Italy by G. Canale and C.S.p.A
Bound in Belgium by Casterman, S.A.

Contents

The rain and us	4
Rainclouds and rainbows	6
Rain is fun!	8
Life-giving rain	10
Animals and birds and the rain	12
Plants and the rain	16
Monsoon and tropical rains	18
Rain and drought	20
Rain and floods	22
Working in the rain	24
Living with the rain	26
Rain and the modern world	28
Glossary	30
Books to read	30
Notes for parents and teachers	31
Index	32

Words that appear in **bold** in the text are explained in the glossary on page 30

The rain and us

These people are hurrying home in the rain in Japan. Many people prefer to stay indoors when it's rainy weather. In towns, pavements are slippery and rain splashes up from cars and buses. In the country, lanes and fields become muddy. Rainy days are often dull days but rain is refreshing. Do you like the rain?

We sometimes complain about rainy weather when it stops us doing what we want to do. Outdoor sports may be delayed or cancelled, like the tennis match these people were watching at Wimbledon. No one likes rain on a sports day, a wedding day or a holiday. Have you ever had a holiday spoiled by rain?

Rainclouds and rainbows

These clouds are dark and heavy with rain. Warm air rises and as it cools, moisture in the clouds forms droplets. These stick together until they are cold and heavy enough to fall as rain. Thunder and lightning sometimes warn us that a rain storm is coming. Thunderclouds can carry large raindrops, so they often produce heavy rain.

We see rainbows when it's rainy and sunny at the same time. This is because raindrops separate the colours of the **spectrum** which make up sunlight. It's best to stand with your back to the sun and look towards the falling rain to see a rainbow clearly.

Rain is fun!

Rainy weather can be fun! Imagine splashing through deep puddles in waterproof boots, or hiding in a den while the rain drums on the roof and trickles down outside. Rain makes different sounds, beating on window panes or gurgling in gutters, and creates patterns on water. What do you like about the rain?

In rainy weather, we wear special waterproof clothes to protect us. Waterproofed fabrics like shiny plastics, waxed cottons and oilskins let the rain slide off. **Sou'westers** and umbrellas keep the rain off our heads. Rubber boots help to keep our feet dry.

Life-giving rain

People, animals and plants need rain to stay alive. The water in rivers and lakes, and from taps in the kitchen all comes from rain. We need water to drink and to wash in. Even the water in these fountains comes from the rain. Think of all the ways you use water during the day. It all comes from the rain!

Rainwater is collected and stored in **reservoirs**. The water is cleaned and purified before being piped to taps in our homes. When no rain falls for a long time, the water in many reservoirs may get low or even dry up. This is why it is important to save water, especially in dry weather.

Animals and birds and the rain

Animals and birds need rain for drinking and bathing. Ducks love splashing about in the rain. **Amphibians** like frogs need the rain to keep their skins moist. Animals living in hot countries, like elephants, enjoy cooling themselves in the rain, but dogs and cats don't like getting wet!

Some animals and birds try to protect their young from the rain. This baby African elephant is sheltering under its mother, during a heavy rain shower in Amboseli National Park, Kenya.

Animals and birds and the rain

Most animals don't like the rain very much. This young mountain gorilla is looking very sad! Does the rain make you feel sad?

These monkeys are called langurs. They are huddling together to keep warm during a downpour in India. They don't look very happy either!

Birds hide in the trees or under bushes when it rains. They keep warm by puffing up their feathers to trap body heat. This grey heron (right) is sitting on its eggs in the rain. The spoonbill (below) has spread its wings to keep the rain off its chicks.

Plants and the rain

In the **desert**, there may be little or no rain. Cacti survive by storing rainwater in their thick, fleshy stems. When rain comes, it can be sudden and heavy, causing floods. Seeds which have remained **dormant** for years burst into life, as in the Kalahari Desert above.

Plants need rain to live and to grow. They combine rainwater with **carbon dioxide** from the air to make the sugars needed for growth. The plant takes rain from the soil through its roots. In parts of the world where there is plenty of rain, the countryside is lush and green because plants can grow easily.

Monsoon and tropical rains

How much rain we get depends on where we live. Some parts of the world have rain all year round. Deserts have little or no rain. Other regions have rainy and dry seasons. In India, there is a rainy summer season, called the wet **monsoon**. This picture shows the monsoon in India when it rains very heavily.

Tropical rain forests have lots of rain all year round. **Tropical** plants have large, glossy leaves which allow the rain to slide off easily. The leaves also have pointed tips so that the rain can drip off. The plants and animals in the rain forests are all adapted to the hot, wet climate.

Rain and drought

Many parts of the world suffer from **drought** during periods of hot, dry weather. Sometimes people have to fetch their own water if their normal supply dries up, as at this waterhole in India. In the dry region of Brazil (below), men collect water from an artificial lake and then sell the water.

In countries where seasonal rains fail, there is danger of drought and **famine**. Without rain, crops will die and people and animals may starve. These cattle have died from lack of food and water in the Sahara Desert in Africa.

Even in countries like Britain, where there is usually lots of rain, we can still get droughts. Without rain, **reservoirs** dry up and parks and gardens become **parched.** To save water, people may be banned from using hosepipes and some houses may lose their tap supply.

Rain and floods

Too much rain brings danger of flooding. Violent storms or heavy seasonal rains can cause rivers to swell and burst their banks, flooding the land. People and animals may be drowned and crops ruined. Homes and property may also be damaged, or even swept away by the floods.

Floods can happen unexpectedly in many parts of the world after heavy rain. Storms can bring several inches of rain in a day. Roads may become flooded and cars stranded. The photographs below show floods in the USA.

Working in the rain

During the growing season, crops need lots of rain. If no rain falls, the farmers must water their crops. Sometimes, they need to avoid rainy weather, when they are spraying their crops or bringing in the harvest.

Rice is the world's most important food crop and it can't grow without plenty of rain. The photograph below shows people working in the flooded rice fields of Indonesia.

Many people's jobs are affected by the rain. Driving is difficult in rainy weather, which can cause poor **visibility**. People who work outdoors like builders and house-painters need to plan work for wet or dry weather. Fishermen are used to working in open boats in the rain.

Living with the rain

Modern architects and designers have found new ways of beating the rain. Some leisure centres now have all-weather domes so that it is warm and dry for holiday-makers all year round.

All-weather surfaces, which do not get muddy and slippery in the rain, have been designed for sports like football and horse-racing.

In countries like Indonesia, where heavy rain can bring danger of flooding, houses are specially adapted. They may be raised above the ground on stilts so that floodwater cannot reach into the doors or windows. They have steeply pitched roofs which allow the heavy rain to run off.

Rain and the modern world

Waste gases, from power stations and car exhausts, dissolve in rain water, turning rain into an acid. Acid rain kills trees, poisons lakes and damages crops. The German forest in this photograph has been damaged by acid rain.

Acid rain can eat into the stonework of buildings. This stone sculpture in Cracow, Poland, has been damaged by acid rain.

This man is restoring a building that has holes in it caused by acid rain. He is using a mixture of sand and cement.

Glossary

Amphibians Animals which live both on land and in water, e.g. frogs, newts.
Carbon dioxide A gas found in air, formed from carbon and oxygen.
Desert A dry region on Earth.
Dormant Resting, not active.
Drought A long period of dry weather when no rain falls.
Famine Extreme shortage of food, leading to hunger and starvation.
Monsoon A wind which changes direction with the seasons, and may bring rain.
Parched Very dry.

Reservoir A lake made by people for storing water.
Sou'wester A rainhat which covers the head and neck.
Spectrum The colours which together make up white sunlight: red, orange, yellow, green, blue, indigo and violet.
Tropical Belonging to the Tropics, the very warm areas either side of the Equator on the Earth's surface.
Tropical rain forest A tropical forest growing in a region of heavy rainfall.
Visibility Conditions for seeing distant objects.

Books to read

Bramwell, Martyn **Weather** (Franklin Watts 1987)
Gribbin, John and Gribbin, Mary **Weather** (Macdonald 1985)
Lambert, David and Hardy, Ralph **Weather and its Work** (Orbis 1988)

Potter, Tony **Factfinders Weather** (BBC Books 1989)
Steele, Philip **Rain** (Weather Watch Series, Franklin Watts 1991)
Taylor, Barbara **Water and Life** (Science Starters, Franklin Watts 1990)

Notes for parents and teachers

This series looks at four aspects of the weather with an interesting and informative approach. The specially chosen photographs reflect the author's innovative style involving the children directly with the subject. The clear and straight-forward text allows children to use the books independently, as a means for reference and as a resource.

All the books in the series relate closely to the National Curriculum offering support to any child embarking on Key Stage 2. Yet those children exploring the weather at home, can enjoy the many exciting ideas and photographs that invite discussion and question from any child.

Suggestions for extension activities

1 Make your own rain gauge by using a funnel in a container that has been marked in mm. Measure daily rainfall and keep a record of it in a weather diary. See if your diary of the weather matches the weather forecasts you see on the television.

2 Study the sky to see the different kinds of cloud. How good can you get at predicting the rainfall by looking at the clouds?

3 Collect sayings and rhymes that tell you about the rain. Find out where they came from and how they originated. Do any of them seem to be true?

Picture acknowledgements
The publishers would like to thank the following for allowing their photographs to be reproduced in this book: Cephas 4 (Nigel Blythe); Bruce Coleman Ltd 10 (Jeremy Grayson), 11 (above/Chris James), 14 (top/Bob Campbell), 14 (below/J. Zwaenepoel), 15 (above/Frank Greenaway), 15 (below/Udo Hirsch), 16 (Norbert Rosing), 17 (top/Gerald Cubitt), 20 (below/L. Marigo), 21 (centre/Peter Ward), 22 (above/Alain Compost), 23 (above/Gerhard Egger), 23 (below/Keith Gunnar), 28 (Hans Reinhard); Chris Fairclough 9 (below), 11 (below), 21 (outside), 24 (Jonathan Smith), 25 (both), 26; Jimmy Holmes 12 (below), Oxford Scientific Films Ltd 6 (Stan Osolinski), 12 (above/Waina Cheng), 13 (Steve Turner), 17 (middle/Michael Fogden), 19 (above/Breck Kent), 19 (below/Deni Brown), 22 (below/David Cayless); Tony Stone Worldwide 29, ZEFA *cover*, 5 (outside), 7, 8, 9 (above), 11 (middle), 17 (below), 18, 20 (above), 27.

Index

Acid rain 28, 29
Amphibians 12

Birds 12, 15
Brazil 20
Britain 21

Cacti 16
Carbon dioxide 17
Clouds 6
Country 4

Desert 16, 21
Driving 25
Drought 20, 21
Ducks 12

Elephants 12, 13

Famine 21
Farmers 24
Fishermen 25

Floods 16, 22, 23, 27
Fountains 10
Frogs 12

Gorilla 14
Gurgling 8

Harvest 24
Heron 15

India 18, 20
Indonesia 27

Japan 4

Kenya 13

Leisure centres 26
Lightning 6

Monkeys 14
Monsoon 18

Muddy 4, 26

Oilskins 9

Patterns 8
Plants 10, 17, 19
Puddles 8

Rainbows 7
Rain forests 19
Reservoirs 11
Rubber boots 9

Soil 17
Sou'westers 9
Spectrum 7
Spoonbill 15
Storms 6, 22, 23
Sunlight 7

Taps 10, 11
Thunder 6